Success With

Addition, Subtraction, Multiplication & Division

SCHOLASTIC

Editor: Ourania Papacharalambous
Cover design by Tannaz Fassihi; cover illustration by Kevin Zimmer
Interior design by Mina Chen
Interior illustrations by Gabriele Tafuni (6-7, 9-11, 14, 16-19, 22-23, 26, 28-29, 33, 36);
Mette Engel (21, 37-41, 45); Doug Jones (24, 44)

ISBN 978-1-338-79831-9
Scholastic Inc., 557 Broadway, New York, NY 10012
Copyright © 2022 Scholastic Inc.
All rights reserved. Printed in the U.S.A.
First printing, January 2022
1 2 3 4 5 6 7 8 9 10   40   29 28 27 26 25 24 23 22

INTRODUCTION

Parents and teachers alike will find *Scholastic Success With Addition, Subtraction, Multiplication & Division* to be a valuable educational tool. It is designed to help students in the fourth grade improve their math skills. The practice pages incorporate challenging puzzles, inviting games, and picture problems that children are sure to enjoy. Children are challenged to sharpen their addition, subtraction, multiplication, and division skills, handle money, and solve story problems. Remember to praise children for their efforts and successes!

TABLE OF CONTENTS

Grade-Appropriate Skills Covered in Scholastic Success With Addition, Subtraction, Multiplication & Division: Grade 4

Apply properties of operations as strategies to add, subtract, multiply and divide.

Fluently add and subtract multi-digit whole numbers using the standard algorithm.

Solve multistep word problems posed with whole numbers and having whole-number answers using the four operations, including problems in which remainders must be interpreted.

Interpret products of whole numbers, e.g., interpret 5×7 as the total number of objects in 5 groups of 7 objects each.

Interpret whole-number quotients of whole numbers, e.g., interpret $56 \div 8$ as the number of objects in each share when 56 objects are partitioned equally into 8 shares, or as a number of shares when 56 objects are partitioned into equal shares of 8 objects each.

Multiply a whole number of up to four digits by a one-digit whole number, and multiply two two-digit numbers, using strategies based on place value and the properties of operations.

Find whole-number quotients and remainders with up to four-digit dividends and one-digit divisors, using strategies based on place value, the properties of operations, and/or the relationship between multiplication and division.

Use multiplication and division within 100 to solve word problems in situations involving equal groups, arrays, and measurement quantities.

Understand division as an unknown-factor problem.

Fluently multiply and divide within 100, using strategies such as the relationship between multiplication and division (e.g., knowing that $8 \times 5 = 40$, one knows $40 \div 5 = 8$) or properties of operations.

The Big Cheese

Add.

> Always complete the operation inside the parentheses ( ) first. Then, complete the rest of the problem.
> $7 + (3 + 6) = 7 + 9 = 16$
> $(4 + 4) + 8 = 8 + 8 = 16$

1. $(7 + 2) + 4 = $ _____

2. $(5 + 4) + 9 = $ _____

3. $8 + (3 + 5) = $ _____

4. $(2 + 6) + (5 + 2) = $ _____

5. $(3 + 3) + (5 + 4) = $ _____

6. $(6 + 6) + 3 = $ _____

7. $5 + (4 + 8) = $ _____

8. $(2 + 9) + 8 = $ _____

9. $(8 + 5) + 4 = $ _____

10. $(8 + 2) + (3 + 2) = $ _____

11. $(2 + 5) + (5 + 8) = $ _____

$(3 + 4) + 7 = $ _____

$9 + (2 + 3) = $ _____

$6 + (2 + 4) = $ _____

$(5 + 1) + (4 + 4) = $ _____

$(4 + 3) + (6 + 2) = $ _____

$4 + (5 + 4) = $ _____

$(3 + 7) + 7 = $ _____

$5 + (5 + 5) = $ _____

$(9 + 3) + 2 = $ _____

$(5 + 7) + (4 + 4) = $ _____

$(6 + 5) + (7 + 4) = $ _____

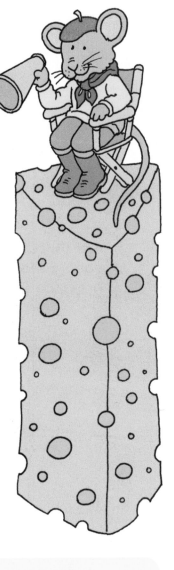

The director ordered a big piece of cheese for each actor in the movie. He ordered 6 pieces from Charlie's Cheese Shop, 3 pieces from Holes and More, and 7 pieces from Mouse Munchers. How many pieces of cheese did the director order in total? Write a number sentence using parentheses to solve the problem.

A-Mazing Eighteen

The answer to an addition problem is called the **sum**.

Add. Find the path that leads from the mouse to the cheese by following the sums of 18.

(5 + 4) + (3 + 6)	(7 + 6) + 5	(5 + 6) + (4 + 2)	(7 + 5) + 7	3 + (7 + 5)
4 + (6 + 6)	3 + (8 + 7)	(5 + 3) + (3 + 4)	(4 + 6) + 5	(5 + 9) + 3
(9 + 2) + 6	(5 + 3) + (6 + 4)	2 + (8 + 8)	8 + (6+ 2)	(4 + 5) + (2 + 5)
5 + (6 + 6)	(6 + 6) + (4 + 6)	(2 + 3) + (9 + 4)	3 + (7 + 5)	(6 + 7) + 6
(7 + 8) + 2	5 + (4 + 6)	7 + (4 + 7)	(5 + 6) + (4 + 3)	(8 + 4) + 6

On another sheet of paper, write a number sentence with 18 as the sum. Do not use a number sentence from above.

Climbing High

To add multiple-digit numbers without regrouping, follow these steps.

1. Add the ones column.
2. Add the tens column.
3. Add the hundreds column.
4. Continue working through each column in order.

Add.

1

1,136	9,025	5,670	5,597
+ 2,433	+ 851	+ 1,312	+ 3,402

2

8,730	2,928	3,650	80,662
+ 1,252	+ 5,021	+ 4,210	+ 11,136

3

55,100	60,439	81,763	36,034
+ 31,892	+ 30,310	+ 8,231	+ 41,753

4

321,957	623,421	264,870
+ 260,041	+ 151,441	+ 303,120

5

594,604	127,094
+ 102,335	+ 832,502

Reaching New Heights

To add multiple-digit numbers with regrouping, follow these steps.

1. Add the ones column.
2. If the sum is greater than 9, regroup to the tens column.
3. Add the tens column.
4. If the sum is greater than 9, regroup to the hundreds column.
5. Continue working through each column in order.

Which of these mountains is the tallest? To find out, add. The sum with the greatest number in each row shows the height of the mountain in feet. Circle the height for each mountain. Then, circle the picture of the tallest mountain.

Kilimanjaro

1

7,542	9,830	6,905	4,671
+ 8,439	+ 9,510	+ 3,492	+ 4,319

Mount Cook

2

5,594	3,642	4,863	5,677
+ 6,624	+ 8,546	+ 7,066	+ 5,307

Denali

3

10,375	12,575	18,408	8,754
+ 8,615	+ 4,192	+ 1,902	+ 8,217

Mount Ebrus

4

13,825	13,257	8,251	9,060
+ 3,934	+ 2,727	+ 6,236	+ 9,450

Find the sum of the heights of the two tallest mountains on this page.

Wild Birds

Some addition problems will require regrouping several times. The steps look like this.

1. Add the ones column. Regroup if needed.	2. Add the tens column. Regroup if needed.	3. Add the hundreds column. Regroup if needed.	4. Continue working through each column in order.
1	11	111	1111
37,462	37,462	37,462	37,462
+ 22,798	+ 22,798	+ 22,798	+ 22,798
0	60	260	60,260

Add. Then, use the code to finish the fun fact below.

bald eagle

Z 953 + 418   B 295 + 337   R 418 + 793   Q 565 + 957   S 862 + 339   X 478 + 283

falcon

I 2,428 + 6,679   C 1,566 + 2,487   Y 3,737 + 6,418   A 9,289 + 4,735   G 8,754 + 368

vulture

L 57,854 + 45,614   P 29,484 + 46,592   E 36,238 + 46,135   F 67,139 + 25,089

owl

D 240,669 + 298,727   O 476,381 + 175,570   R 882,948 + 176,524

What do all of these birds have in common?

They are ___ ___ ___ ___ ___   ___ ___
632 9,107 1,211 539,396 1,201   651,951 92,228

___ ___ ___ ___.
76,076 1,059,472 82,373 10,155

The American Bald Eagle

To add numbers that require regrouping in more than one column, follow these steps.

1. Add the ones column. Regroup if needed.
2. Add the tens column. Regroup if needed.
3. Add the hundreds column. Regroup if needed.
4. Continue working through each column in order.

Add. Then, use the code to finish the fun fact below.

H
$$8,754 + 368$$

L
$$7,789 + 4,759$$

I
$$8,997 + 9,978$$

A
$$8,599 + 8,932$$

E
$$5,476 + 4,846$$

O
$$9,475 + 7,725$$

C
$$8,838 + 9,668$$

T
$$6,867 + 7,256$$

M
$$9,891 + 3,699$$

N
$$92,854 + 37,898$$

U
$$25,748 + 85,362$$

Y
$$99,977 + 82,943$$

R
$$57,544 + 78,587$$

The bald eagle is found ___ ___ ___ ___ ___ ___
17,200 130,752 12,548 182,920   17,200 130,752

___ ___ ___ ___ ___ ___ ___ ___
14,123 9,122 10,322   130,752 17,200 136,131 14,123 9,122

___ ___ ___ ___ ___ ___ ___ ___
17,531 13,590 10,322 136,131 18,975 18,506 17,531 130,752

___ ___ ___ ___ ___ ___ ___ ___ ___ .
18,506 17,200 130,752 14,123 18,975 130,752 10,322 130,752 14,123

Funny Bone

Add. Then, use the code to find the answer
to the riddle.

Use the same steps to
add several addends.
Some columns will
require regrouping,
and some will not.

W	T	P	N	O	E
1,233 1,442 + 5,226	6,314 3,380 + 2,606	2,305 2,404 + 2,439	1,238 6,281 + 5,366	3,541 309 + 7,845	3,525 2,213 + 9,281

H	R	S	!	A	U
444 7,283 + 8,217	4,327 4,331 + 1,746	4,024 678 + 4,505	5,441 421 + 3,954	2,653 3,338 + 2,924	5,560 4,202 + 1,541

What is the difference between a man and a running dog?

11,695 12,885 15,019   7,901 15,019 8,915 10,404 9,207

12,300 10,404 11,695 11,303 9,207 15,019 10,404 9,207 ,

12,300 15,944 15,019   11,695 12,300 15,944 15,019 10,404

7,148 8,915 12,885 12,300 9,207 9,816

Canine Calculations

The numbers being added together are called **addends**.

Use the sum to help you find the missing numbers of each addend.

1

```
  1 1
  6, 7 4 □            9, 4 4 3         □, 5 □ 8          □, 2 2 7
+ □, 3 8 2          + 9, □ 1 □        + 5, 3 6 1        + 6, □ 7 3
─────────           ─────────         ─────────         ─────────
1 0, 1 2 3          1 9, 2 6 0          9, 9 3 9          9, 2 0 0
```

2

```
      1                  1                1                 1
  3, 8 4 1            7, 0 □ 4        □, □ 1 0          □, 4 2 6
+ □, 0 6 □          + 9, □ 3 8        + 9, 3 8 5        + 7, 9 2 □
─────────           ─────────         ─────────         ─────────
  7, 9 0 5          1 6, 4 6 2        1 9, 1 9 5        1 5, 3 4 9
```

3

```
  1 1                1 1              1 1                 1
  1, 7 □ 3            3, □ 5 4        □, 2 8 4          8, 8 6 □
+    □ 5 8          + 6, 4 □ 4        + 3, □ 2 1        + □, 3 1 7
─────────           ─────────         ─────────         ─────────
  1, 9 3 1          1 0, 1 2 8          8, 1 0 5        1 1, 1 8 0
```

4

```
  1 1 1              1     1          1 1 1              1   1
  3, □ 4 □            □, 7 □ 9        7, 5 5 □          4, □ 9 5
+ 9, 2 □ 5          + 8, □ 2 □        + □, □ 4 8        + □, 6 □ 8
─────────           ─────────         ─────────         ─────────
1 3, 2 1 3          1 8, 4 8 3        1 7, 5 0 6        1 1, 2 2 3
```

Wag'n Tail Kennels bought two enormous bags of dog treats. One bag had 38,□69 dog treats in it. The other bag had 4□,510 pieces of dog treats. Altogether the bags had 80,879 treats. On another sheet of paper, find the number of dog treats in each bag.

A Penny Saved Is a Penny Earned

Write a number sentence for each problem. Solve.

1 Aimee and her 2 sisters are saving to buy a camera. Aimee has $12.89. Each of her sisters has $28.53. How much money do all the girls have combined?

2 Katie has $23.95 in her purse, $17.23 in her bank, and $76.82 in her savings account. What is the total the amount of Katie's money?

3 Jonah worked in the yard for 3 days. The first day he earned $7.96. The second day he earned $2.00 more than the first day. The third day he earned $2.00 less than the first day. How much did Jonah earn altogether?

4 Jack has $9.29. He also has 79 dimes and 139 pennies. How much money does he have altogether?

5 Kelsey has 478 coins in her collection. The silver dollars equal $79.00 and the quarters equal $99.75. How much is Kelsey's collection worth in all?

6 Claire bought lemonade for herself and two friends. Each cup costs $1.75. How much did Claire spend in all?

 On another sheet of paper, write a word problem with a sum equal to $41.68.

Reach for the Stars

Always complete the operation inside the parentheses ( ) first.
Then, complete the rest of the problem.

$(18 - 9) - 3 =$ _____ $18 - (9 - 3) =$ _____
$9 - 3 = 6$ $18 - 6 = 12$

Subtract. Then, use the code to answer the question below.

N $(16 - 8) - 5 =$ _____

B $11 - (6 - 4) =$ _____

U $(23 - 4) - 5 =$ _____

D $(12 - 3) - (16 - 7) =$ _____

L $(17 - 5) - (12 - 8) =$ _____

W $13 - (11 - 3) =$ _____

R $(22 - 6) - 5 =$ _____

I $(21 - 1) - (16 - 12) =$ _____

H $(11 - 3) - 4 =$ _____

T $(18 - 6) - 2 =$ _____

L $19 - (10 - 6) =$ _____

E $(13 - 5) - (10 - 9) =$ _____

O $(14 - 7) - (12 - 6) =$ _____

I $(16 - 8) - (11 - 9) =$ _____

D $17 - (14 - 9) =$ _____

N $(21 - 2) - (15 - 9) =$ _____

O $(10 - 3) - (11 - 6) =$ _____

How many stars are in the Milky Way Galaxy?

___ ___ ___ ___ ___ ___ ___ ___ ___ ___
10   5   1   4   14 13   0 11   7 12

___ ___ ___ ___ ___ ___ ___
9   16   8   15   6   2   3

Moon Madness

Subtract. Then, write the differences in order
to answer the fun fact.

The answer to
a subtraction
problem is called
the **difference**.

How fast does the moon travel in its orbit?

____ ____ ____ ____ m.p.h.

1. $11 - (15 - 9) =$ _____

2. $(15 - 7) - (11 - 5) =$ _____

3. $16 - (15 - 8) =$ _____

4. $15 - (15 - 8) =$ _____

5. $(13 - 9) - (11 - 8) =$ _____

6. $12 - (13 - 6) =$ _____

7. $(17 - 9) - (13 - 8) =$ _____

8. $18 - (13 - 4) =$ _____

9. $14 - (13 - 5) =$ _____

10. $12 - (18 - 9) =$ _____

11. $14 - (18 - 9) =$ _____

12. $17 - (14 - 6) =$ _____

13. $18 - (16 - 7) =$ _____

14. $(16 - 8) - (10 - 4) =$ _____

15. $13 - (14 - 7) =$ _____

16. $17 - (12 - 3) =$ _____

17. $(15 - 6) - (12 - 5) =$ _____

18. $16 - (17 - 9) =$ _____

19. $15 - (16 - 8) =$ _____

20. $(20 - 7) - (6 - 2) =$ _____

On another sheet of paper, write subtraction problems with a code to
answer this question: *What is the diameter of the moon?* (2,160 miles)
Have a friend solve the problems.

Chess, Anyone?

To subtract multiple-digit numbers without regrouping, follow these steps.

1. Subtract the ones column.

```
  6,48|9|
-  2,16|5|
       |4|
```

2. Subtract the tens column.

```
  6,4|8|9
-  2,1|6|5
      |2|4
```

3. Subtract the hundreds column.

```
  6,|4|89
-  2,|1|65
     |3|24
```

4. Subtract the thousands column.

```
  |6|,489
- |2|,165
  |4|,324
```

Subtract.

6,518 − 1,414	9,842 − 621	7,966 − 3,234	6,549 − 21
4,916 − 4,113	8,385 − 7,224	3,309 − 203	5,977 − 2,863
9,459 − 300	7,749 − 7,637	4,969 − 2,863	3,496 − 3,260
6,839 − 5,324	1,578 − 1,241	8,659 − 46	9,481 − 9,240

Checkmate

To subtract with regrouping, follow these steps.

1. Subtract the ones column. Regroup if needed.

```
  2 1 1
  4 3 Y
- 2 6 6
───────
      5
```

2. Subtract the tens column. Regroup if needed.

```
    1 2
  3 2 1 1
    4 3 Y
  - 2 6 6
─────────
      6 5
```

3. Subtract the hundreds column. Regroup if needed.

```
    1 2
  3 2 1 1
    4 3 Y
  - 2 6 6
─────────
    1 6 5
```

Subtract. Cross out the chess piece with the matching difference. The last piece standing is the winner. Write the number of the winning piece in the box below.

464

416

 73

240

506

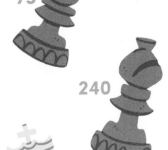

119

```
  956        239        842
- 492      - 176      - 426
```

```
  153        351        983
-  80      - 172      - 284
```

```
  526        643        258
- 286      - 479      - 139
```

```
  932        852
- 426      - 476
```

☐ is left standing.

63

179

164

699

479

376

Out of the Park!

To subtract with regrouping, follow these steps.

1.
```
        5 10
  3,4 6̸ 0̸
-   8 7 6
─────────
          4
```

2.
```
         15
      3 8̸ 10
  3,4̸ 6̸ 0̸
-    8 7 6
─────────
        8 4
```

3.
```
      13 15
   2 3̸ 8̸ 10
  3̸,4̸ 6̸ 0̸
-    8 7 6
─────────
      5 8 4
```

4.
```
      13 15
   2 3̸ 8̸ 10
  3̸,4̸ 6̸ 0̸
-    8 7 6
─────────
  2,5 8 4
```

Subtract. Then, use the code to solve the riddle below.

E
```
  4,622
- 1,284
```

E
```
  5,198
-   469
```

H
```
  3,469
-   890
```

B
```
  7,603
- 3,728
```

T
```
  6,077
- 1,258
```

A
```
  9,617
-   759
```

R
```
  3,804
-   115
```

I
```
  2,972
-   984
```

H
```
  8,941
- 1,895
```

N
```
    952
-    95
```

C
```
  7,263
- 4,772
```

E
```
  9,550
- 4,298
```

L
```
  6,451
-   868
```

S
```
  2,850
- 1,976
```

In what part of the ballpark do you find the whitest clothes?

___ ___   ___ ___ ___
1,988 857   4,819 2,579 5,252

___ ___ ___ ___ ___ ___ ___ ___ ___!
3,875 5,583 4,729 8,858 2,491 7,046 3,338 3,689 874

On another sheet of paper, write a subtraction problem that requires
regrouping two times. Ask someone at home to solve it.

Touchdown!

Subtract. The final score of the game will be written in the footballs at the bottom of the page.

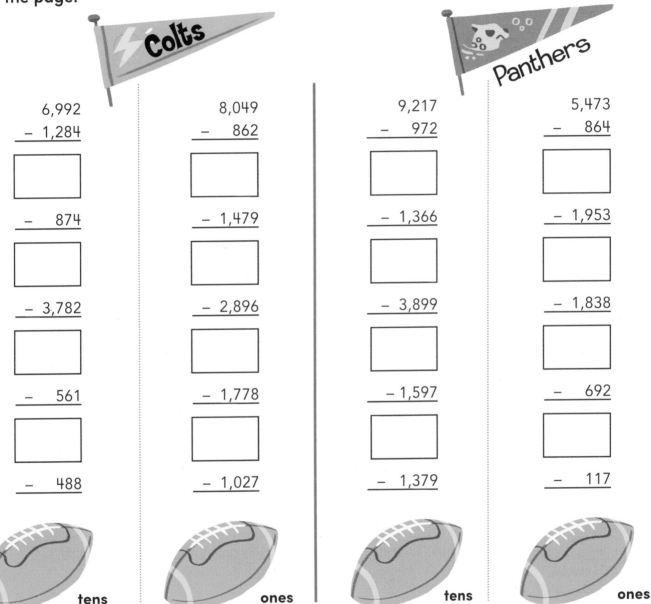

Colts

```
  6,992
- 1,284
_____
[      ]

-   874
_____
[      ]

- 3,782
_____
[      ]

-   561
_____
[      ]

-   488
_____
```
tens

```
  8,049
-   862
_____
[      ]

- 1,479
_____
[      ]

- 2,896
_____
[      ]

- 1,778
_____
[      ]

- 1,027
_____
```
ones

Panthers

```
  9,217
-   972
_____
[      ]

- 1,366
_____
[      ]

- 3,899
_____
[      ]

- 1,597
_____
[      ]

- 1,379
_____
```
tens

```
  5,473
-   864
_____
[      ]

- 1,953
_____
[      ]

- 1,838
_____
[      ]

-   692
_____
[      ]

-   117
_____
```
ones

Who won? _____

On another sheet of paper, write a series of four subtraction problems that have a final difference equal to your age.

A Funny Fixture

Subtract. Then, use the code to find the answer
to the riddle.

> If necessary, continue regrouping into the ten thousands column.

E 63,210 − 11,799	**I** 41,392 − 38,164	**R** 76,146 − 34,982	**E** 12,388 − 9,891
P 54,391 − 23,689	**H** 68,612 − 59,446	**T** 97,413 − 89,608	**L** 32,602 − 19,561
A 18,546 − 11,798	**G** 92,475 − 76,097	**S** 29,816 − 17,909	**!** 78,752 − 69,275

Why did the tired man climb up the chandelier?

,

___ ___ ___   ___
9,166 51,411 11,907   6,748

___ ___ ___ ___ ___
13,041 3,228 16,378 9,166 7,805

___ ___ ___ ___ ___ ___ ___ ___
11,907 13,041 2,497 51,411 30,702 2,497 41,164 9,477

Bright Idea!

Find each missing subtrahend by subtracting the
difference from the minuend.

Each part of a
subtraction problem
has a name:

3,460 ← minuend
- 876 ← subtrahend
   84 ← difference

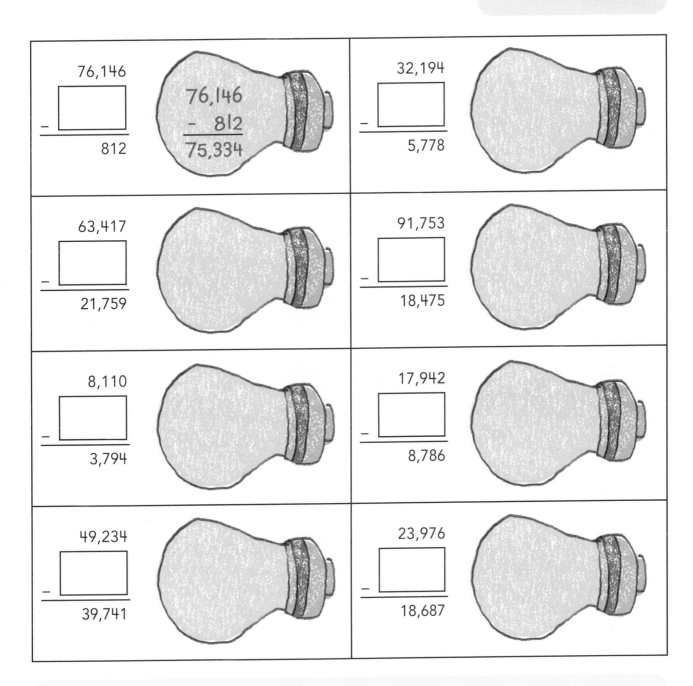

76,146
- ☐
812

76,146
-   812
75,334

32,194
- ☐
5,778

63,417
- ☐
21,759

91,753
- ☐
18,475

8,110
- ☐
3,794

17,942
- ☐
8,786

49,234
- ☐
39,741

23,976
- ☐
18,687

On another sheet of paper, write two subtraction problems with missing
subtrahends. Ask a friend to solve the problems.

Sums & Differences

Point-scoring in the Intergalactic Football League
Touchdown .... 6 points
Touchdown with an extra point............................. 7 points
Touchdown with a 2-point conversion .... 8 points
Field Goal... 3 points

The Asteroids played the Constellations. Each team scored a field goal in the first quarter. In the second quarter, the Asteroids scored a touchdown, but missed the extra point. At the half, the Constellations led by 1 point. In the third quarter, the Asteroids made a touchdown with the extra point. The Constellations matched them, and made a field goal, as well. In the fourth quarter, following a Constellations field goal, the Asteroids scored a touchdown with a 2-point conversion.

Who won? _____

By what score? _____

Point-scoring in the Intergalactic Basketball League
consists of 1-point free throws, 2-point goals, 3-point goals, and 4-point goals (those made without looking at the basket!)

The Comets, playing the Meteors, led 22–9 at the end of the first quarter. They led by 7 at the half after scoring two 4-point goals, two 3-point goals, four 2-point goals and four free throws. In the third quarter, the Meteors had six 2-point goals and four free throws. They also had one more 4-point goal, but one less 3-point goal than the Comets. The Comets had five 2-point goals and no free-throws. They scored 20 points in the quarter. In the last quarter, each team scored the same number of 4-point, 3-point, and 2-point goals. The Comets scored 31 points in that quarter, including four free throws. The Meteors made two fewer free throws than the Comets.

Who won? _____

By what score? _____

Road Trip!

Write a number sentence for each problem. Solve.

1 Hannah's family drove 1,246 miles in 2 days. They drove 879 miles the first day. How far did they drive the second day?

2 Joplin is between Wells and Greenville. The distance from Wells to Greenville is 4,128 miles. The distance from Wells to Joplin is 1,839 miles. How far is it from Joplin to Greenville?

3 The Midnight Express travels 6,283 miles total. When the train reaches Springfield, it has traveled 2,496 miles. How much farther will the Midnight Express travel?

4 Jacob's scout troop is going camping 947.6 miles from home. The bus breaks down after 289.9 miles. How far is the bus from the campgrounds?

5 Jonesburgh is between Johnsonville and Piper. Johnsonville is 8,612 miles from Piper. Piper is 4,985 miles from Jonesburgh. How far is it from Jonesburgh to Johnsonville?

6 Lola's family drove 2,391 miles to go to the beach. They drove home using another route that was 3,290 miles. How much longer was the second route?

It's a Circus in Here!

To multiply is to use repeated addition. Basic multiplication facts are learned by memorizing.

3 groups of 5 = 5 + 5 + 5 = 3 x 5 = 15

2	3	9	5	6
× 2	× 3	× 6	× 4	× 7

6	4	5	9	2
× 4	× 1	× 8	× 3	× 4

8	9	1	3	9
× 6	× 5	× 0	× 5	× 7

8	4	9	0	3
× 8	× 7	× 9	× 8	× 4

5	6	7	5	8
× 5	× 6	× 7	× 2	× 4

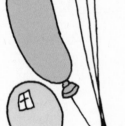

On another sheet of paper, draw a picture to match this problem: There are 6 clowns. Each clown is holding 7 balloons. Then, write the multiplication fact that tells the total number of balloons.

Under the Big Top

Multiply. Then, use each product and the code to
answer the riddles.

The answer to a
multiplication problem is
called the **product**. The
numbers being multiplied
are called **factors**.

A = 12	G = 40	M = 36	S = 64	Y = 25
B = 27	H = 24	N = 72	T = 45	Z = 2
C = 5	I = 48	O = 42	U = 0	
D = 56	J = 4	P = 16	V = 21	
E = 18	K = 54	Q = 28	W = 49	
F = 81	L = 8	R = 63	X = 1	

What happened to the human cannonball at the circus?

___ ___   ___ ___ ___   ___ ___ ___ ___ ___
4 × 6   6 × 3   7 × 7   3 × 4   8 × 8   8 × 3   6 × 8   7 × 9   2 × 9   8 × 7

___ ___ ___   ___ ___ ___ ___ ___   ___ ___
6 × 2   8 × 9   7 × 8   9 × 9   8 × 6   9 × 7   3 × 6   8 × 7   7 × 6   9 × 8

___ ___ ___   ___ ___ ___ ___   ___ ___ ___!
5 × 9   6 × 4   9 × 2   8 × 8   4 × 3   6 × 6   6 × 3   8 × 7   2 × 6   5 × 5

What happened to the kid who ran away with the circus?

___ ___   ___ ___ ___
3 × 8   2 × 9   4 × 6   3 × 4   8 × 7

___ ___   ___ ___ ___ ___ ___
9 × 5   6 × 7   9 × 3   7 × 9   8 × 6   9 × 8   5 × 8

___ ___   ___ ___ ___ ___ ___!
6 × 8   5 × 9   3 × 9   2 × 6   5 × 3   9 × 6

Come to Costa Rica

To multiply with a 2-digit factor, follow these steps.

1. Multiply the ones column.

2. Multiply the bottom factor in the ones column with the top factor in the tens column.

Multiply. Use the code to fill in the blanks below.

I
```
   82
×   4
```

O
```
   91
×   9
```

S
```
   21
×   8
```

H
```
   92
×   3
```

J
```
   73
×   2
```

E
```
   71
×   7
```

L
```
   53
×   3
```

R
```
   90
×   8
```

C
```
   61
×   6
```

N
```
   11
×   5
```

A
```
   32
×   4
```

F
```
   41
×   9
```

T
```
   70
×   7
```

E
```
   52
×   4
```

P
```
   40
×   8
```

| 490 | 276 | 208 |

| 366 | 128 | 320 | 328 | 490 | 128 | 159 |

| 819 | 369 | | 366 | 819 | 168 | 490 | 128 |

| 720 | 328 | 366 | 128 | | 328 | 168 |

| 168 | 128 | 55 | | 146 | 819 | 168 | 497 |

Multiple Ways to Multiply

The **zero property**: Any factor multiplied by 0 always has a product of 0.
$$9 \times 0 = 0$$
The **property of one**: Any factor multiplied by 1 always has a product of the other factor.
$$5 \times 1 = 5$$
The **commutative property**: Changing the order of the factors does not change the product.
$$4 \times 3 = 3 \times 4$$

The **associative property**: Changing how the factors are grouped does not change the product.
$$(5 \times 2) \times 6 = 5 \times (2 \times 6)$$
The **distributive property**: Multiplying a factor by the sum of two numbers equals the sum of the two products.
$$6 \times (2 + 5) = (6 \times 2) + (6 \times 5)$$

Identify each property and then solve.

1 _____ $5 \times 6 = 6 \times 5$

$5 \times 11 = \boxed{} \times \boxed{}$ $4 \times \boxed{} = 12 \times \boxed{}$ $\boxed{} \times \boxed{} = 7 \times 6$

$\boxed{} \times 9 = \boxed{} \times 3$ $8 \times 10 = \boxed{} \times \boxed{}$ $2 \times \boxed{} = 5 \times \boxed{}$

2 _____ $3 \times (2 + 5) = (3 \times 2) + (3 \times 5)$

$6 \times (4 + 5) = (6 \times \boxed{}) + (6 \times \boxed{})$ $7 \times (\boxed{} + \boxed{}) = (7 \times 5) + (7 \times 8)$

$9 \times (3 + 7) = (9 \times \boxed{}) + (9 \times \boxed{})$ $\boxed{} \times (5 + 8) = (3 \times 5) + (3 \times 8)$

3 _____ $135 \times 0 = 0$

$18 \times \boxed{} = 0$ $3 \times 0 = \boxed{}$ $\boxed{} \times 11 = 0$ $9 \times \boxed{} = 0$ $8 \times 0 = \boxed{}$

$7 \times 0 = \boxed{}$ $15 \times \boxed{} = 0$ $0 \times 6 = \boxed{}$ $8 \times \boxed{} = 0$ $\boxed{} \times 9 = 0$

4 _____ $3 \times (2 \times 4) = (3 \times 2) \times 4$

$6 \times (2 \times 3) = (\text{_____}) \times 3$ $\boxed{} \times (4 \times 9) = (6 \times 4) \times 9$

$8 \times (12 \times 2) = (\text{_____}) \times 2$ $(5 \times 2) \times 3 = 5 \times (\text{_____})$

A Faraway Country

To multiply with a 2-digit factor that requires regrouping, follow these steps.

1. Multiply the ones.
   Regroup if needed.
   7 x 3 = 21

2. Multiply the bottom factor in the ones column with the top factor in the tens column. Add the extra tens.
   6 x 3 = 18   18 + 2 = 20

   2 0 1

Multiply.

1.
```
    48          24          73
  x  3        x  7        x  4
```

2.
```
    57          63          56
  x  7        x  9        x  3
```

3.
```
    98          64          57          35          23          82
  x  2        x  8        x  8        x  9        x  8        x  6
```

4.
```
    95          77          83          96          28          96
  x  9        x  6        x  9        x  8        x  4        x  5
```

Norway is known for its thousands of islands, rugged coastline, and fjords (long narrow inlets with steep cliffs). One famous fjord is Preikestolen, with a cliff that is nearly flat on top. To find out how many meters high it is, add the products in row 1 on another sheet of paper.

A Multiplication Puzzler

Multiply. Circle each product in the puzzle. The products will go across and down.

①
$$\begin{array}{r} 32 \\ \times\ 8 \\ \hline \end{array}$$
$$\begin{array}{r} 56 \\ \times\ 8 \\ \hline \end{array}$$
$$\begin{array}{r} 70 \\ \times\ 5 \\ \hline \end{array}$$
$$\begin{array}{r} 65 \\ \times\ 4 \\ \hline \end{array}$$
$$\begin{array}{r} 68 \\ \times\ 5 \\ \hline \end{array}$$

②
$$\begin{array}{r} 81 \\ \times\ 3 \\ \hline \end{array}$$
$$\begin{array}{r} 89 \\ \times\ 6 \\ \hline \end{array}$$
$$\begin{array}{r} 60 \\ \times\ 5 \\ \hline \end{array}$$
$$\begin{array}{r} 69 \\ \times\ 4 \\ \hline \end{array}$$
$$\begin{array}{r} 96 \\ \times\ 2 \\ \hline \end{array}$$

③
$$\begin{array}{r} 49 \\ \times\ 6 \\ \hline \end{array}$$
$$\begin{array}{r} 78 \\ \times\ 4 \\ \hline \end{array}$$
$$\begin{array}{r} 72 \\ \times\ 8 \\ \hline \end{array}$$
$$\begin{array}{r} 68 \\ \times\ 9 \\ \hline \end{array}$$
$$\begin{array}{r} 24 \\ \times\ 9 \\ \hline \end{array}$$

④
$$\begin{array}{r} 43 \\ \times\ 5 \\ \hline \end{array}$$
$$\begin{array}{r} 97 \\ \times\ 3 \\ \hline \end{array}$$
$$\begin{array}{r} 91 \\ \times\ 2 \\ \hline \end{array}$$
$$\begin{array}{r} 79 \\ \times\ 3 \\ \hline \end{array}$$
$$\begin{array}{r} 49 \\ \times\ 3 \\ \hline \end{array}$$

6	1	2	9	6	8	2	3	7
9	3	6	3	1	4	7	2	3
7	1	2	5	6	0	6	1	5
2	8	3	0	9	5	4	5	7
6	2	4	3	2	3	2	1	0
0	7	4	3	4	0	6	9	3
1	6	8	1	3	3	1	2	0
7	5	2	9	1	0	4	3	5
5	3	4	3	8	0	2	9	4

Scholastic Success With Addition, Subtraction, Multiplication & Division • Grade 4

The Big City

To multiply with a 3-digit factor that requires regrouping, follow these steps.

1. Multiply the ones. Regroup if needed.

```
    1
  473
x   6
    8
```

2. Multiply the tens in the top factor. Add the extra tens. Regroup if needed.

```
   41
  473
x   6
   38
```

3. Multiply the hundreds in the top factor. Regroup if needed.

```
   41
  473
x   6
2,838
```

Multiply.

1

```
  463        923        194        630        494        606
x   3      x   4      x   8      x   5      x   2      x   4
```

2

```
  325        817        293        168        208        196
x   7      x   6      x   9      x   3      x   8      x   6
```

3

```
  305        815        980        155        626        126
x   2      x   5      x   7      x   9      x   3      x   6
```

 A subway train travels 296 miles daily. How far does the train travel in a week?

A Changing Reef

To multiply with zeros, follow these steps.

90 x 2	9 x 2 = 18 Add a zero in the ones place to make 180	90 x 20	9 x 2 = 18 Add 2 zeros—one in the ones place, and one in the tens place.	900 x 20	9 x 2 = 18 Add 3 zeros—one in the ones place, one in the tens place, and one in the hundreds place

Multiply.

 1

80 x 7	60 x 50	900 x 30	40 x 11	120 x 2	200 x 60

 2

70 x 7	120 x 300	60 x 90	700 x 60	50 x 70	30 x 12

3

600 x 80	40 x 12	30 x 8	90 x 50	200 x 120	50 x 8

fringing reef

barrier reef

atoll

The formation of a coral reef starts growing around the top of an undersea volcano, forming a fringing reef. As the volcano sinks, it leaves behind a barrier reef. When the volcano sinks below the ocean's surface, an atoll is left. On another sheet of paper, write three problems with products to match those on the pictures.

Stallions in the Stable

Multiply. Use the products to put each stallion back where he belongs. Write the horse's name on the stall door.

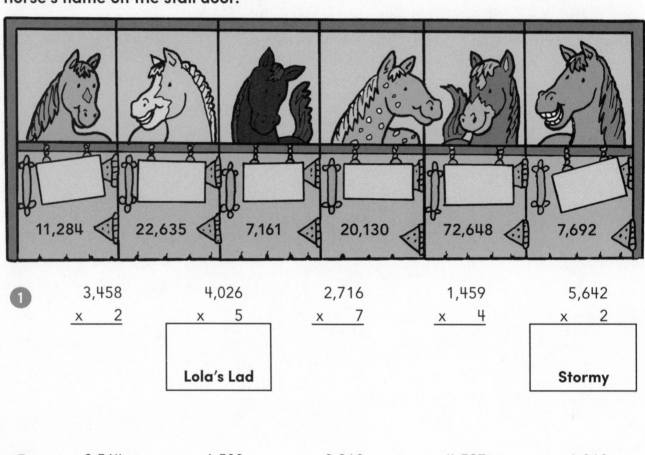

| 11,284 | 22,635 | 7,161 | 20,130 | 72,648 | 7,692 |

1

3,458	4,026	2,716	1,459	5,642
x 2	x 5	x 7	x 4	x 2
	Lola's Lad			**Stormy**

2

2,564	1,508	9,210	4,527	1,018
x 3	x 6	x 9	x 5	x 8
Thunder			**Sunrise**	

3

1,809	2,387	9,081	7,186	7,130
x 7	x 3	x 8	x 4	x 6
	Midnight	**Lightning**		

Stop Horsing Around!

To multiply with a 2-digit factor that requires regrouping, follow these steps.

1. Multiply the ones digit.

```
    3
   46
 x 26
  276
```

2. Place a zero in the ones column.

```
    3
   46
 x 26
  276
    0
```

3. Multiply by the tens digit.

```
  1
  3
   46
 x 26
  276
+ 920
```

4. Add to find the product.

```
  1
  3
   46
 x 26
  276
+ 920
1,196
```

Multiply. Then, use the code to answer the riddle below.

G 32 × 48

T 67 × 14

S 53 × 27

I 96 × 52

A 83 × 33

D 49 × 72

M 39 × 28

E 56 × 15

N 83 × 24

R 75 × 46

K 96 × 51

H 84 × 62

What horses like to stay up late?

____ ____ ____ ____ ____ ____ ____ ____ ____ ____!
1,992 4,992 1,536 5,208 938 1,092 2,739 3,450 840 1,431

Famous Landmarks

Which of these landmarks is the tallest? Multiply. Write the ones digit of each product in order to find the height of each landmark. Circle the tallest landmark.

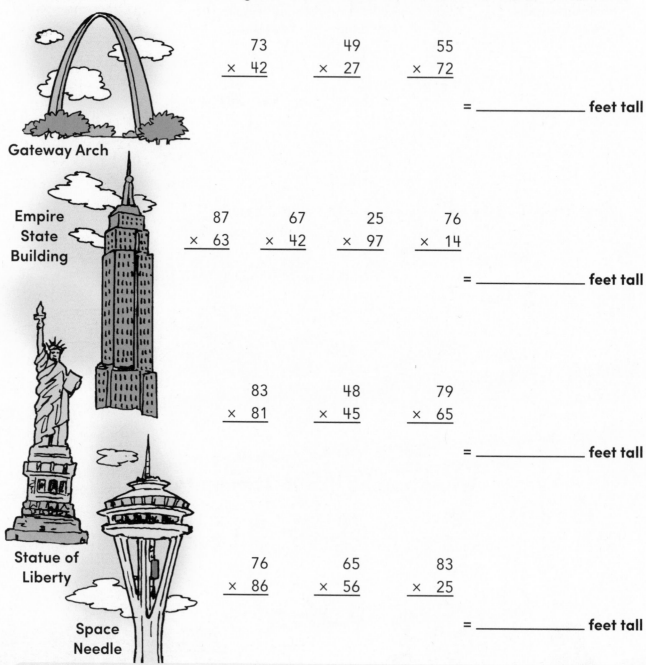

Gateway Arch

$$\begin{array}{r} 73 \\ \times\ 42 \\ \hline \end{array} \qquad \begin{array}{r} 49 \\ \times\ 27 \\ \hline \end{array} \qquad \begin{array}{r} 55 \\ \times\ 72 \\ \hline \end{array}$$

= _____ feet tall

Empire
State
Building

$$\begin{array}{r} 87 \\ \times\ 63 \\ \hline \end{array} \qquad \begin{array}{r} 67 \\ \times\ 42 \\ \hline \end{array} \qquad \begin{array}{r} 25 \\ \times\ 97 \\ \hline \end{array} \qquad \begin{array}{r} 76 \\ \times\ 14 \\ \hline \end{array}$$

= _____ feet tall

$$\begin{array}{r} 83 \\ \times\ 81 \\ \hline \end{array} \qquad \begin{array}{r} 48 \\ \times\ 45 \\ \hline \end{array} \qquad \begin{array}{r} 79 \\ \times\ 65 \\ \hline \end{array}$$

= _____ feet tall

Statue of
Liberty

$$\begin{array}{r} 76 \\ \times\ 86 \\ \hline \end{array} \qquad \begin{array}{r} 65 \\ \times\ 56 \\ \hline \end{array} \qquad \begin{array}{r} 83 \\ \times\ 25 \\ \hline \end{array}$$

Space
Needle

= _____ feet tall

The Willis Tower in Chicago is 110 stories tall. If 55 people work on each floor, how many total people work in the building? Write the problem and answer on another sheet of paper.

Monumental Multiplication

Multiply.

1

| 362 | 602 | 452 | 283 | 918 | 473 |
| x 43 | x 18 | x 22 | x 13 | x 27 | x 55 |

2

| 540 | 417 | 308 |
| x 38 | x 56 | x 61 |

3

| 692 | 586 | 918 |
| x 34 | x 37 | x 86 |

4

| 467 | 598 | 861 |
| x 42 | x 29 | x 73 |

The Washington Monument has 897 steps. If 42 people climb to the top, how many steps have they climbed altogether? Write the problem and answer on another sheet of paper.

The Music Store

When a multiplication problem involves money, the product must have a dollar sign and a decimal point. The decimal point is placed between the ones digit and the tenths digit.

```
    6
    2
  $3.71
x    94
  14.84
+333.90
$348.74
```

Remember to use a dollar sign and a decimal point.

Multiply. Then, use the code to answer the riddle below.

N $1.94 x 23

M $0.79 x 25

I $2.06 x 64

O $0.68 x 45

A $3.68 x 32

T $9.54 x 19

F $0.88 x 72

D $0.93 x 94

E $8.15 x 67

S $7.43 x 92

R $0.87 x 75

H $6.92 x 83

Where do musicians buy instruments?

$117.76 $181.26 $181.26 $574.36 $546.05

$63.36 $131.84 $63.36 $546.05 $117.76 $44.62 $87.42

$ 87.42 $131.84 $19.75 $546.05 $683.56 $181.26 $30.60 $65.25 $546.05 !

The Corner Candy Store

Write a number sentence for each problem. Solve.

Word problems that suggest equal groups often require multiplication.

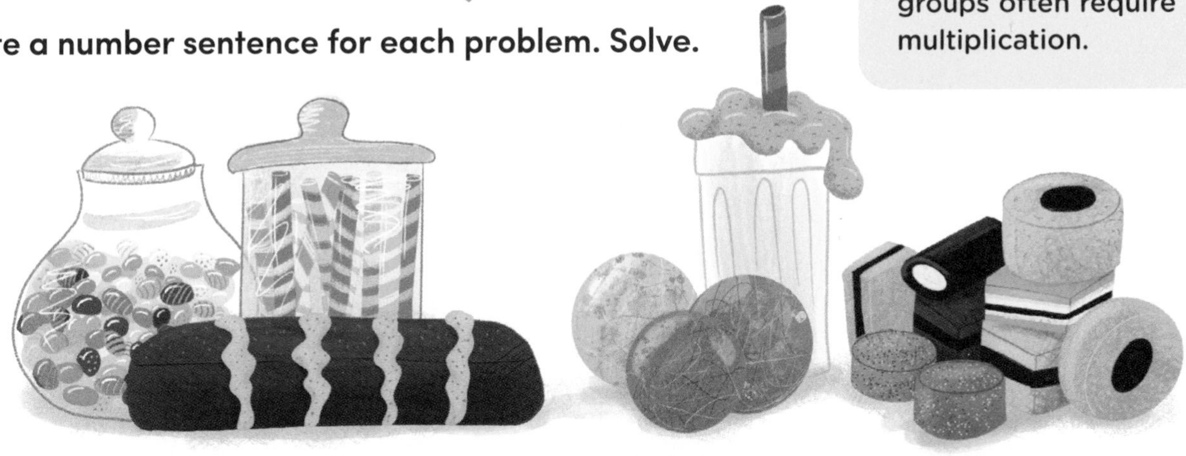

1 Sam bought 4 candy bars at $1.55 each. How much did Sam spend altogether?	4 Mr. Johnson ordered 48 boxes of jawbreakers. Each box contained 392 pieces of candy. How many jawbreakers did Mr. Johnson order?
2 Carly's mom sent her to the candy store with 29 party bags. She asked Carly to fill each bag with 45 pieces of candy. How many pieces of candy will Carly buy?	5 35 children visited the candy store after school. Each child spent 57¢. How much money was spent in all?
3 Mr. Johnson, the owner of the candy store, keeps 37 jars behind the candy counter. Each jar contains 286 pieces of candy. How many pieces of candy are behind the counter altogether?	6 Nick bought each of his 6 friends a milkshake. Each milkshake cost $2.98. How much did Nick spend in all?

What's on TV?

To divide means to make equal groups. Since multiplication also depends on equal groups, you can use multiplication facts to help you learn division facts.

$$8 \times 6 \to 48 \quad \to \quad 8 \atop 6 \overline{)48}$$

Divide.

1. $4\overline{)24}$ $4\overline{)36}$ $7\overline{)56}$ $5\overline{)25}$ $9\overline{)81}$ $8\overline{)24}$

2. $5\overline{)45}$ $8\overline{)72}$ $4\overline{)28}$ $6\overline{)42}$ $6\overline{)36}$ $1\overline{)9}$

3. $3\overline{)12}$ $7\overline{)21}$ $6\overline{)48}$ $3\overline{)24}$ $8\overline{)32}$ $7\overline{)63}$

4. $8\overline{)64}$ $7\overline{)49}$ $5\overline{)30}$ $9\overline{)27}$ $6\overline{)6}$ $3\overline{)15}$

Divide to learn an interesting fact.

In what year was television invented?

$3\overline{)3}$ $8\overline{)72}$ $7\overline{)14}$ $8\overline{)64}$

 Research to find the year something else was invented. On another sheet of paper, write four division facts with the year hidden in their quotients.

Monitor Division

Each part of a division problem has a name.

$$8 \leftarrow \text{quotient}$$
$$\text{divisor} \rightarrow 6\overline{)48} \leftarrow \text{dividend}$$

Divide.

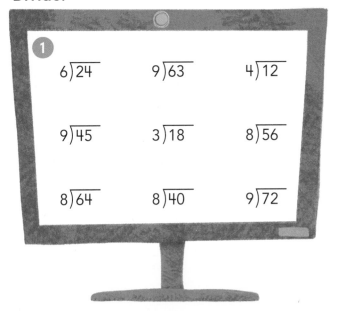

1

$6\overline{)24}$ $9\overline{)63}$ $4\overline{)12}$

$9\overline{)45}$ $3\overline{)18}$ $8\overline{)56}$

$8\overline{)64}$ $8\overline{)40}$ $9\overline{)72}$

2

$7\overline{)35}$ $9\overline{)36}$ $7\overline{)21}$

$4\overline{)32}$ $5\overline{)20}$ $6\overline{)36}$

$3\overline{)9}$ $7\overline{)56}$ $9\overline{)81}$

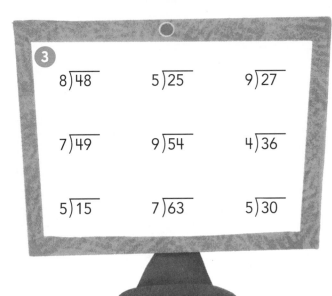

3

$8\overline{)48}$ $5\overline{)25}$ $9\overline{)27}$

$7\overline{)49}$ $9\overline{)54}$ $4\overline{)36}$

$5\overline{)15}$ $7\overline{)63}$ $5\overline{)30}$

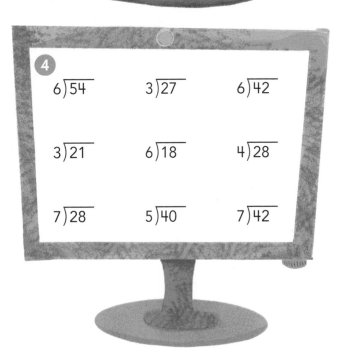

4

$6\overline{)54}$ $3\overline{)27}$ $6\overline{)42}$

$3\overline{)21}$ $6\overline{)18}$ $4\overline{)28}$

$7\overline{)28}$ $5\overline{)40}$ $7\overline{)42}$

On another sheet of paper, write nine division facts with a quotient of 8.

A Barrel of Numbers

To divide with zeros, follow these examples.

```
      80   64 ÷ 8 = 8                      800   64 ÷ 8 = 8
 8 )640    0 ÷ 8 = 0                  8 )6400    0 ÷ 8 = 0
           Add a zero to make 80.               0 ÷ 8 = 0
                                                Add 2 zeros to make 800.
```

Divide

1   6)420   9)8100   6)540   5)4500   3)2400

2   3)1800   4)320   8)7200   7)560   5)400

3   3)150   4)360   6)4800   6)360   8)640

 On another sheet of paper, write three problems with quotients to match those on the barrels.

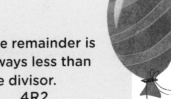

No Way!

To divide with remainders, follow these steps.

1. Does 8 x _ = 34? No!

$$8 \overline{)34}$$

2. Use the closest smaller dividend.
8 x 4 = 32

$$8 \overline{)34} \atop 32$$ (4)

3. Subtract to find the remainder.

$$\begin{array}{r} 4 \\ 8 \overline{)34} \\ -32 \\ \hline 2 \end{array}$$

4. The remainder is always less than the divisor.

$$\begin{array}{r} 4R2 \\ 8 \overline{)34} \\ -32 \\ \hline 2 \end{array}$$

Divide. Then, use the code to complete the riddle below.

E $9\overline{)84}$	L $3\overline{)29}$	S $7\overline{)67}$	O $5\overline{)24}$
T $6\overline{)23}$	N $6\overline{)47}$	P $6\overline{)41}$	I $7\overline{)52}$
O $4\overline{)19}$	A $8\overline{)70}$	T $3\overline{)26}$	S $9\overline{)55}$
H $4\overline{)23}$	! $7\overline{)45}$	R $5\overline{)27}$	N $8\overline{)79}$

Emily: Yesterday, I saw a man at the mall with very long arms. Every time he went up the stairs, he stepped on them.

Jack: Wow! He stepped on his arms?

Emily:

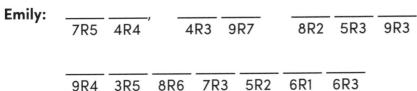

___ ___ , ___ ___   ___ ___ ___
7R5 4R4   4R3 9R7   8R2 5R3 9R3

___ ___ ___ ___ ___ ___ ___
9R4 3R5 8R6 7R3 5R2 6R1 6R3

Mousing Around

To divide with a 3-digit dividend, follow these steps.

1.
$$7\overline{)427}$$
    6
    42
    7 x ___ = 42
    7 x 6 = 42

2.
$$7\overline{)427}$$
    6
    - 42↓
    07
    Subtract.
    Bring down the digit.

3.
$$7\overline{)427}$$
    61
    - 42↓
    07
    - 7
    0
    7 x ___ = 7
    7 x 1 = 7
    Subtract.

Divide. Then, use the code to answer the riddle below.

T 4)208   U 6)306   H 9)819   C 3)246   A 4)368

E 8)648   O 7)497   S 4)248   N 2)168   D 4)288

C 4)328   I 3)159   W 5)305   M 9)279   ! 4)88

Why did the cat hang out near the computer?

___ ___   ___ ___ ___ ___ ___ ___   ___ ___
53 52   61 92 84 52 81 72   52 71

___ ___ ___ ___ ___   ___ ___ ___
82 92 52 82 91   52 91 81

___ ___ ___ ___ ___ ___
31 71 51 62 81 22

On another sheet of paper, design a mouse pad. Include at least three division problems and their quotients in your design.

Surfing the Web

When the divisor has a remainder in the middle of a problem, follow these steps.

1.
```
     10
  8)816
    80
```
8 x ___ = 81
8 x 10 = 80

2.
```
     10
  8)816
   -80↓
     16
```
Subtract.

Bring down the digit.

3.
```
     102
  8)816
   -80↓
     16
    -16
      0
```
8 x ___ = 16
8 x 2 = 16

Subtract again.

Divide. Use another piece of paper to work on the problems. Then, connect each problem to its answer to learn the definitions of some computer terms.

1 5)375 **browser**

2 6)492 **byte**

3 2)216 **download**

4 3)249 **gigabyte**

5 9)243 **Internet**

6 8)288 **megabyte**

7 4)424 **network**

8 6)564 **program**

9 7)532 **scanner**

10 4)312 **virus**

11 9)486 **website**

82 amount of data equal to 8 bits

75 a program to help get around the Internet

54 a collection of linked information presented as text, visuals, or other multimedia format

106 a group of computers linked together so they can share information

36 an amount of information equal to 1,048,576 bytes

27 a worldwide system of linked computers

108 to transfer information from a host computer to a personal computer

83 an amount of information equal to 1,024 megabytes

78 a program that damages other programs and data

94 instructions for a computer to follow

76 a device that can transfer words and pictures from a printed page into the computer

Poolside!

Divide. Then, use the code to answer the riddle below.

O 4)258   **G** 7)445   **K** 6)573   **R** 9)380

L 8)419   **A** 9)748   **M** 5)293

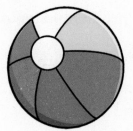

P 8)706   **S** 3)263   **T** 6)356   **C** 7)309

What kind of pool is not made for swimming?

___ ___ ___ ___ ___ ___ ___ ___ !
83R1   44R1 83R1 42R2 88R2 64R2 64R2 52R3

Bone Up on Division

To divide by a 2-digit divisor, follow these steps.

1.
$$15\overline{)330}$$
  2
  30

15 x ___ = 30
Use the closest
smaller dividend.
15 x 2 = 30
Put the 2 above
the 3 tens.

2.
  2
$$15\overline{)330}$$
  - 30
   30

Subtract.
Bring down
the ones digit.

3.
  22
$$15\overline{)330}$$
  - 30
   30
  - 30
    0

15 x ___ = 30
15 x 2 = 30

Subtract again.

Divide. Write the digit in the ones place with the least amount in each row to find out how many bones an adult human body has.

1. $13\overline{)559}$ $16\overline{)208}$ $39\overline{)468}$ $23\overline{)874}$

2. $31\overline{)682}$ $46\overline{)690}$ $26\overline{)858}$ $47\overline{)940}$

3. $35\overline{)630}$ $27\overline{)486}$ $28\overline{)756}$ $18\overline{)828}$

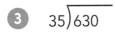 ___ ___ ___ **bones**

 About how many bones are in a newborn baby's body? Divide to find out:
7,500 ÷ 25 = _____.

Let's Go to the Show

Look at each example to learn how to finish dividing when there is a zero in the quotient.

1.
$$\begin{array}{r} 306 \\ 8\overline{)2448} \\ -24 \\ \hline 04 \\ -\ 0 \\ \hline 48 \\ -48 \end{array}$$

2.
$$\begin{array}{r} 680 \\ 6\overline{)4080} \\ -36 \\ \hline 048 \\ -48 \\ \hline 00 \end{array}$$

3.
$$\begin{array}{r} 20R9 \\ 44\overline{)889} \\ -88 \\ \hline 09 \\ -\ 0 \\ \hline 9 \end{array}$$

Divide. Then, use the code to answer the riddle below.

S 3)1812   **U** 4)3632   **W** 18)910   **X** 25)3250

G 17)356   **B** 6)1848   **R** 39)786   **J** 8)7216

A 7)4207   **E** 27)562   **Y** 9)2880   **T** 9)6345

What is the name of the movie about toads in outer space?

___ ___ ___ ___   ___ ___ ___ ___ ___!
604 705 601 20R6   50R10 601 20R6 705 604

Imagine that you have popped 1,422 pieces of popcorn for you and your five friends. How many pieces would each person get? Write the problem and answer on another sheet of paper.

ANSWER KEY

Page 5
1. 13, 14 **2.** 18, 14 **3.** 16, 12 **4.** 15, 14
5. 15, 15 **6.** 15, 13 **7.** 17, 17 **8.** 19, 15
9. 17, 14 **10.** 15, 20 **11.** 20, 22
Extra Activity: 16 pieces of cheese.
Number sentence may be (6+3) + 7 or
6 + (3 + 7).

Page 6

18	18	17	19	15
16	18	15	15	17
17	18	18	16	16
17	22	18	15	19
17	15	18	18	18

Extra Activity: Answers may vary.

Page 7
1. 3,569; 9,876; 6,982; 8,999
2. 9,982; 7,949; 7,860; 91,798
3. 86,992; 90,749; 89,994; 77,787
4. 581,998; 774,862; 567,990
5. 696,939; 959,596

Page 8
1. 15,981; (19,340) 10,397; 8,990
2. (12,218) 12,188; 11,929; 10,984
3. 18,990; 16,767; (20,310) 16,971
4. 17,759; 15,984; 14,487; (18,510)
Denali is the highest mountain listed.
Extra Activity: 39,650 feet

Page 9
Z. 1,371 **B.** 632 **R.** 1,211 **Q.** 1,522
S. 1,201 **X.** 761 **I.** 9,107 **C.** 4,053
Y. 10,155 **A.** 14,024 **G.** 9,122 **L.** 103,468
P. 76,076 **E.** 82,373 **F.** 92,228
D. 539,396 **O.** 651,951 **R.** 1,059,472
THEY ARE BIRDS OF PREY.

Page 10
H. 9,122 **L.** 12,548 **I.** 18,975 **A.** 17,531
E. 10,322 **O.** 17,200 **C.** 18,506 **T.** 14,123
M. 13,590 **N.** 130,752 **U.** 111,110
Y. 182,920 **R.** 136,131
**THE BALD EAGLE IS FOUND ONLY ON
THE NORTH AMERICAN CONTINENT.**

Page 11
W. 7,901 **T.** 12,300 **P.** 7,148 **N.** 12,885
O. 11,695 **E.** 15,019 **H.** 15,994 **R.** 10,404
S. 9,207 **!.** 9,816 **A.** 8,915 **U.** 11,303
**ONE WEARS TROUSERS, THE OTHER
PANTS!**

Page 12
1. 6,741 + 3,382 = 10,123;
9,443 + 9,817 = 19,260;
4,578 + 5,361 = 9,939;
2,227 + 6,973 = 9,200
2. 3,841 + 4,064 = 7,905;
7,024 + 9,438 = 16,462;
9,810 + 9,385 = 19,195;
7,426 + 7,923 = 15,349
3. 1,773 + 158 = 1,931;
3,654 + 6,474 = 10,128;
4,284 + 3,821 = 8,105;
8,863 + 2,317 = 11,180
4. 3,948 + 9,265 = 13,213;
9,759 + 8,724 = 18,483;
7,558 + 9,948 = 17,506;
4,595 + 6,628 = 11,223
Extra Activity:
38,369 + 42,510 = 80,879 treats

Page 13
1. 12.89 + 28.53 + 28.53 = $69.95
2. 23.95 + 17.23 + 76.82 = $118
3. 7.96 + 9.96 + 5.96 = $23.88
4. 9.29 + 7.90 + 1.39 = $18.58
5. 79 + 99.75 = $178.75
6. 1.75 + 1.75 + 1.75 = $5.25
Extra Activity: Answers may vary.

Page 14
N. 3 **T.** 10 **B.** 9 **L.** 15 **U.** 14 **E.** 7 **D.** 0
O. 1 **L.** 8 **I.** 6 **W.** 5 **D.** 12 **R.** 11 **N.** 13
I. 16 **O.** 2 **H.** 4
TWO HUNDRED BILLION

Page 15
2,288 mph
1. 5 **2.** 2 **3.** 9 **4.** 8 **5.** 1 **6.** 5 **7.** 3 **8.** 9
9. 6 **10.** 3 **11.** 5 **12.** 9 **13.** 9 **14.** 2 **15.** 6
16. 8 **17.** 2 **18.** 8 **19.** 7 **20.** 9
Extra Activity: Answers may vary.

Page 16
5,104; 9,221; 4,732; 6,528
803; 1,161; 3,106; 3,114
9,159; 112; 2,106; 236
1,515; 337; 8,613; 241

Page 17
464, 63, 416
73, 179, 699
240, 164, 119
506, 376
479 is left standing.

Page 18
E. 3,338 **E.** 4,729 **H.** 2,579 **B.** 3,875
T. 4,819 **A.** 8,858 **R.** 3,689 **I.** 1,988
H. 7,046 **N.** 857 **C.** 2,491 **E.** 5,252
L. 5,583 **S.** 874
IN THE BLEACHERS!
Extra Activity: Answers may vary.

Page 19
First Column: 5,708; 4,834; 1,052; 491; 3
Second Column: 7,187; 5,708; 2,812;
1,034; 7
Third Column: 8,245; 6,879; 2,980;
1,383; 4
Fourth Column: 4,609; 2,656; 818; 126; 9
Panthers
Extra Activity: Answers may vary.

Page 20
E. 51,411 **I.** 3,228 **R.** 41,164 **E.** 2,497
P. 30,702 **H.** 9,166 **T.** 7,805 **L.** 13,041
A. 6,748 **G.** 16,378 **S.** 11,907 **!** 9,477
HE'S A LIGHT SLEEPER!

Page 21
First column: 75,334; 41,658; 4,316;
9,493
Second column: 26,416; 73,278; 9,156;
5,289
Extra Activity: Answers may vary.

Page 22
Asteroids, 24–23
Comets, 99–97

Page 23
1. 1,246 - 879 = 367 miles
2. 4,128 - 1,839 = 2,289 miles
3. 6,283 - 2,496 = 3,787 miles
4. 947.6 - 289.9 = 657.7 miles
5. 8,612 - 4,985 = 3,627 miles
6. 3,290 - 2,391 = 899 miles

Page 24
4, 9, 54, 20, 42
24, 4, 40, 27, 8
48, 45, 0, 15, 63
64, 28, 81, 0, 12
25, 36, 49, 10, 32
Extra Activity: 6 x 7 = 42 balloons

Page 25
**HE WAS HIRED AND FIRED ON
THE SAME DAY!
HE HAD TO BRING IT BACK!**

Page 26
I. 328 O. 819 S. 168 H. 276 J. 146
E. 497 L. 159 R. 720 C. 366 N. 55
A. 128 F. 369 T. 490 E. 208 P. 320
THE CAPITAL OF COSTA RICA IS SAN JOSÉ.

Page 27
1. The commutative property
5 x 11 = 11 x 5, 4 x 12 = 12 x 4,
6 x 7 = 7 x 6, 3 x 9 = 9 x 3,
8 x 10 = 10 x 8, 2 x 5 = 5 x 2
2. The distributive property
6 x (4 + 5) = (6 x 4) + (6 x 5),
7 x (5 + 8) = (7 x 5) + (7 x 8),
9 x (3 + 7) = (9 x 3) + (9 x 7),
3 x (5 + 8) = (3 x 5) + (3 x 8)
3. The zero property
18 x 0 = 0, 3 x 0 = 0, 0 x 11 = 0,
9 x 0 = 0, 8 x 0 = 0, 7 x 0 = 0,
15 x 0 = 0, 0 x 6 = 0, 8 x 0 = 0,
0 x 9 = 0
4. The associative property
6 x (2 x 3) = (6 x 2) x 3,
6 x (4 x 9) = (6 x 4) x 9,
8 x (12 x 2) = (8 x 12) x 2,
(5 x 2) x 3 = 5 x (2 x 3)

Page 28
1. 144, 168, 292
2. 399, 567, 168
3. 196, 512, 456, 315, 184, 492
4. 855, 462, 747, 768, 112, 480
Extra Activity: 604 meters

Page 29
1. 256, 448, 350, 260, 340
2. 243, 534, 300, 276, 192
3. 294, 312, 576, 612, 216
4. 215, 291, 182, 237, 147

Page 30
1. 1,389; 3,692; 1,552; 3,150; 988; 2,424
2. 2,275; 4,902; 2,637; 504; 1,664; 1,176
3. 610; 4,075; 6,860; 1,395; 1,878; 756
Extra Activity: 2,072 miles

Page 31
1. 560; 3,000; 27,000; 440; 240; 12,000
2. 490; 36,000; 5,400; 42,000; 3,500; 360
3. 48,000; 480; 240; 4,500; 24,000; 400
Extra Activity: Answers may vary.

Page 32
1. 6,916; 20,130; 19,012; 5,836; 11,284
2. 7,692; 9,048; 82,890; 22,635; 8,144
3. 12,663; 7,161; 72,648; 28,744; 42,780
Stormy, Sunrise, Midnight,
Lola's Lad, Lightning, Thunder

Page 33
G. 1,536 T. 938 S. 1,431 I. 4,992
A. 2,739 D. 3,528 M. 1,092 E. 840
N. 1,992 R. 3,450 K. 4,896 H. 5,208
NIGHTMARES!

Page 34
Gateway Arch:
3,066; 1,323; 3,960; 630 feet
Empire State Building:
5,481; 2,814; 2,425; 1,064; 1,454 feet
Statue of Liberty:
6,723; 2,160; 5,135; 305 feet
Space Needle:
6,536; 3,640; 2,075; 605 feet
Empire State Building should be circled.
Extra Activity: 6,050 people

Page 35
1. 15,566; 10,836; 9,944; 3,679; 24,786; 26,015
2. 20,520; 23,352; 18,788
3. 23,528; 21,682; 78,948
4. 19,614; 17,342; 62,853
Extra Activity: 37,674 steps

Page 36
N. $44.62 M. $19.75 I. $131.84
O. $30.60 A. $117.76 T. $181.26
F. $63.36 D. $87.42 E. $546.05
S. $683.56 R. $65.25
H. $574.36
AT THE FIFE AND DIME STORE!

Page 37
1. 4 x 1.55 = $6.20
2. 29 x 45 = 1,305 pieces of candy
3. 37 x 286 = 10,582 pieces of candy
4. 48 x 392 = 18,816 jawbreakers
5. 35 x 0.57 = $19.95
6. 6 x 2.98 = $17.88

Page 38
1. 6, 9, 8, 5, 9, 3
2. 9, 9, 7, 7, 6, 9
3. 4, 3, 8, 8, 4, 9
4. 8, 7, 6, 3, 1, 5
1928
Extra Activity: Answers may vary.

Page 39
1. 4, 7, 3; 5, 6, 7; 8, 5, 8
2. 5, 4, 3; 8, 4, 6; 3, 8, 9
3. 6, 5, 3; 7, 6, 9; 3, 9, 6
4. 9, 9, 7; 7, 3, 7; 4, 8, 6
Extra Activity: Answers may vary.

Page 40
1. 70, 900, 90, 900, 800
2. 600, 80, 900, 80, 80
3. 50, 90, 800, 60, 80
Extra Activity: Answers may vary.

Page 41
E. 9R3 L. 9R2 S. 9R4 O. 4R4
T. 3R5 N. 7R5 P. 6R5 I. 7R3
O. 4R3 A. 8R6 T. 8R2 S. 6R1
H. 5R3 !. 6R3 R. 5R2 N. 9R7
NO, ON THE STAIRS!

Page 42
T. 52 U. 51 H. 91 C. 82 A. 92 E. 81
O. 71 S. 62 N. 84 D. 72 C. 82 I. 53
W. 61 M. 31 !. 22
IT WANTED TO CATCH THE MOUSE!
Extra Activity: Answers may vary.

Page 43
1. 75 **2.** 82 **3.** 108 **4.** 83 **5.** 27 **6.** 36
7. 106 **8.** 94 **9.** 76 **10.** 78 **11.** 54

Page 44
O. 64R2 G. 63R4 K. 95R3 R. 42R2
L. 52R3 A. 83R1 M. 58R3 P. 88R2
S. 87R2 T. 59R2 C. 44R1
A CARPOOL!

Page 45
1. 43, 13, 12, 38 **2.** 22, 15, 33, 20
3. 18, 18, 27, 46
206 bones
Extra Activity: 300 bones

Page 46
S. 604 U. 908 W. 50R10 X. 130
G. 20R16 B. 308 R. 20R6 J. 902
A. 601 E. 20R22 Y. 320 T. 705
STAR WARTS!
Extra Activity: 237 pieces of popcorn